# ANOTHER F★CKING
## Coloring Book

Adams Media

New York   London   Toronto   Sydney   New Delhi

Adams Media
An Imprint of Simon & Schuster, Inc.
100 Technology Center Drive
Stoughton, MA 02072

For information about special discounts for bulk purchases, please contact Simon & Schuster Special Sales at 1-866-506-1949 or business@simonandschuster.com.

The Simon & Schuster Speakers Bureau can bring authors to your live event. For more information or to book an event contact the Simon & Schuster Speakers Bureau at 1-866-248-3049 or visit our website at www.simonspeakers.com.

Interior design by Michelle Roy Kelly
Interior images © iStockphoto.com

Manufactured in the United States of America

11 2022

Library of Congress Cataloging-in-Publication Data has been applied for.

ISBN 978-1-4405-9841-8

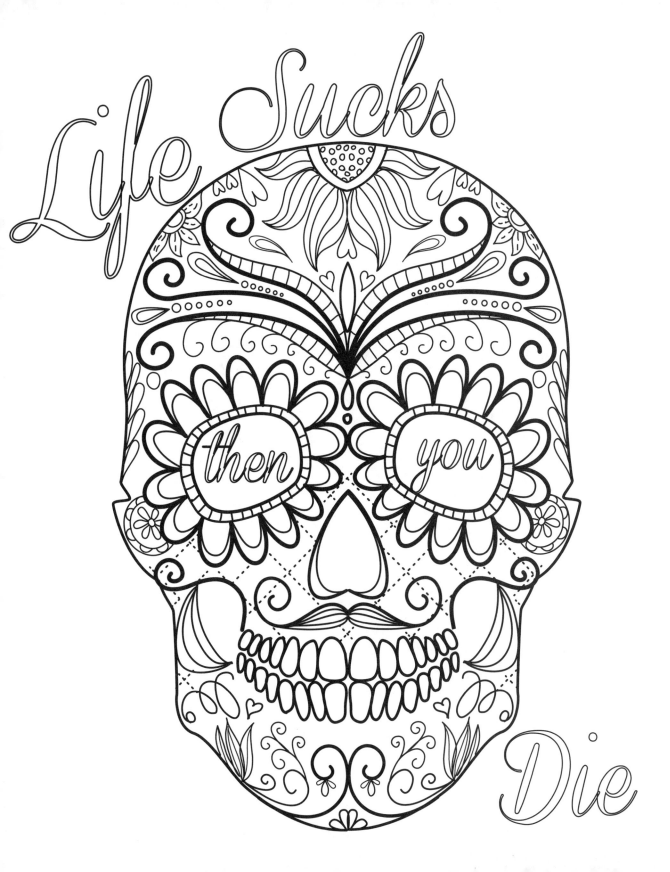

HOME IS WHERE THE LIQUOR IS

# IT'S TEA TIME, BITCHES

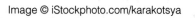

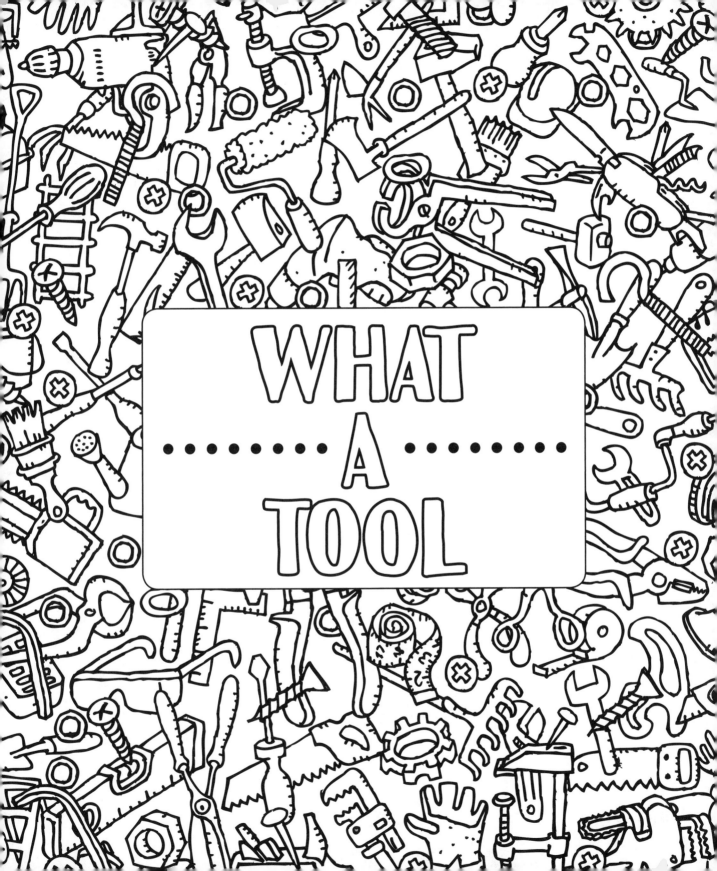

I FARTED

HANG IN
THERE,
ASSHOLE

just
spreading
my seed

NOW THAT'S SOME BULL

UNICORNS ARE FUCKING RAD

PLAYING WITH MY BALLS

I love you like a
fat kid loves cake

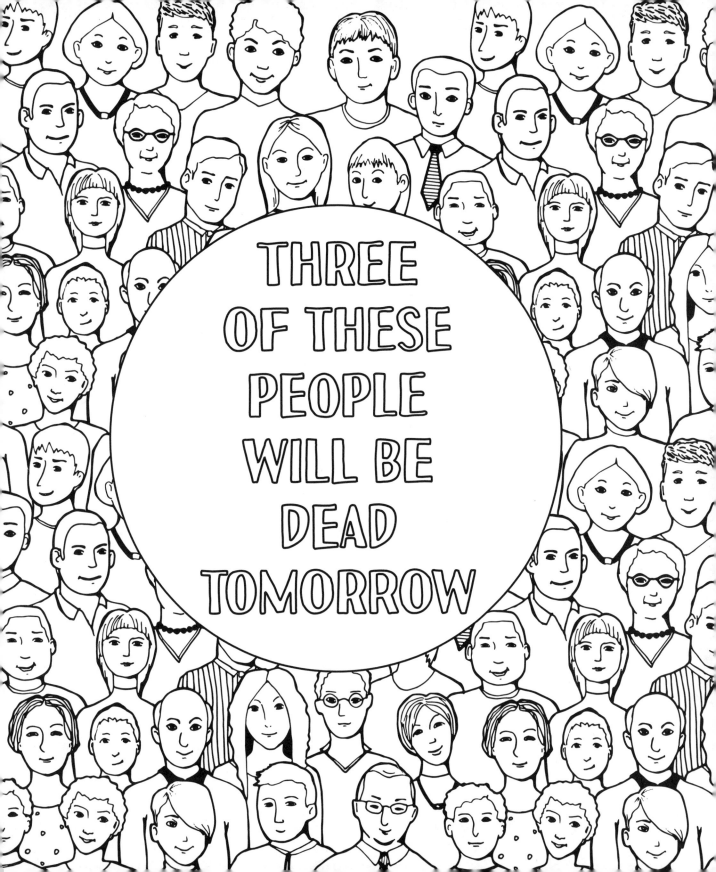

ENJOY YOUR TRIP

# DON'T RAIN ON MY FUCKING PARADE

DRINK LIKE

NO ONE IS WATCHING

your words
are like air
from a colon

# 'SUP BEEYOTCH

in wine there is wisdom, in beer there is freedom, in water there is bacteria